SHEPHERDESS

SHEEP SHEEP SHEEP SHEEP SHEEP SHEEP SHEEP SHEEP
SHEEP SHEEP SHEEP SHEEP SHEEP SHEEP SHEEP SHEEP
SHEEP SHEEP SHEEP SHEEP SHEEP SHEEP SHEEP SHEEP
SHEEP SHEEP SHEEP SHEEP SHEEP SHEEP SHEEP SHEEP
SHEEP SHEEP CROW SHEEP SHEEP SHEEP SHEEP SHEEP
SHEEP SHEEP SHEEP SHEEP SHEEP SHEEP SHEEP SHEEP
SHEEP SHEEP SHEEP SHEEP SHEEP SHEEP SHEEP SHEEP
SHEEP SHEEP SHEEP SHEEP SHEEP SHEEP SHEEP SHEEP
SHEEP SHEEP SHEEP SHEEP SHEEP SHEEP SHEEP SHEEP
SHEEP SHEEP SHEEP SHEEP SHEEP SHEEP RAVEN SHEEP
SHEEP SHEEP SHEEP SHEEP SHEEP SHEEP SHEEP SHEEP
SHEEP SHEEP SHEEP SHEEP SHEEP SHEEP SHEEP SHEEP
SHEEP SHEEP SHEEP SHEEP SHEEP DEER SHEEP SHEEP
SHEEP SHEEP SHEEP SHEEP SHEEP SHEEP SHEEP SHEEP
SHEEP SHEEP SHEEP SHEEP SHEEP SHEEP SHEEP SHEEP
SHEEP SHEEP SHEEP SHEEP SHEEP SHEEP SHEEP SHEEP
SHEEP SHEEP SHEEP SHEEP SHEEP SHEEP SHEEP SHEEP
SHEEP SHEEP SHEEP SHEEP SHEEP SHEEP SHEEP SHEEP
SHEEP SHEEP STRAY DOGS SHEEP SHEEP SHEEP SHEEP
SHEEP SHEEP SHEEP SHEEP SHEEP SHEEP SHEEP SHEEP
SHEEP SHEEP SHEEP SHEEP SHEEP SHEEP SHEEP SHEEP
SHEEP SHEEP SHEEP SHEEP SHEEP SHEEP SHEEP SHEEP
SHEEP SHEEP SHEEP SHEEP SHEEP SHEEP SHEEP SHEEP
SHEEP SHEEP SHEEP SHEEP SHEEP SHEEP SHEEP SHEEP
SHEEP FOX SHEEP SHEEP SHEEP SHEEP SHEEP SHEEP
SHEEP SHEEP SHEEP SHEEP SHEEP SHEEP SHEEP SHEEP
SHEEP SHEEP SHEEP SHEEP SHEEP SHEEP SHEEP SHEEP
SHEEP SHEEP SHEEP SHEEP SHEEP SHEEP SHEEP SHEEP
SHEEP SHEEP SHEEP SHEEP SHEEP SHEEP SHEEP SHEEP
SHEEP SHEEP SHEEP SHEEP FOX SHEEP SHEEP SHEEP
SHEEP SHEEP SHEEP SHEEP SHEEP SHEEP SHEEP SHEEP
SHEEP SHEEP SHEEP SHEEP SHEEP SHEEP SHEEP SHEEP
SHEEP SHEEP SHEEP SHEEP SHEEP SHEEP SHEEP SHEEP
SHEEP SHEEP SHEEP SHEEP SHEEP SHEPHERDESS SHEEP
SHEEP SHEEP SHEEP SHEEP SHEEP SHEEP SHEEP SHEEP

The Call

I throw things together to leave
then see you like a parked car
and before I can stop: *I'm going
to farm-sit sheep, want to come?*
You do and you're grinning
and I tell myself I'm interested
in the way facial expression is a play
of darkness and light, and how
shadow gives meaning.
We are old friends and soon close

to where we met as students, we pass
Preseli bluestones, cross ancient ley lines.
You remind me it's all about magnets.
I like pushing them to their limits.

Preparing for Sheep-Sitting

It's no Bo Peep work, no falling asleep on haystacks.
Leaving you to unpack I step into my shepherd role
before the farmer hands over.

We drag heavy metal hurdles along hard paths,
get tangled in brambles, make a pen in the field.
Today it's the turn of the boy lambs.

They eye us with suspicion, like sheepdogs we circle
round to herd them. In the pen they jostle together
like people on the underground.

The farmer grabs a leg as one leaps from reach.
Docile, my foot, they buck and jump like rodeo sheep,
sometimes headbutt him, wrestle him to the ground.

He checks their eyes, in silence holds out a hand.
I pass the wormer and it's squirted into unwilling mouths,
to some he gives a shot from the syringe.

My job then to let them go, one by one. They fight
against freedom. As if only we know what's good
for them. Wander off as if all that fuss was for show.

Lessons in Shepherding

It's so wet the sheep are learning to swim.
These are not ordinary sheep, not woolly,
they have black bellies.
In the morning they watch me
with amber eyes and breath-clouds.

I clear the ice. It drops to the grass,
shatters in the weak March sun.
You appear, encroaching their flight zone,
and the ewes scatter.
Sheep make you nervous.

You become the egg-collector,
scour brambles for nests,
lock up the hens at night.
They are Cream Legbar,
their eggs pale blue.
Henpecking is rife.
Feathers are everywhere.
I watch a hen eyeing an egg:
she jerks forward, nudges it,
pecks and pecks until
she cracks it. Eats it.

Then you come towards me,
smiling, as if going to kiss me,
but there's blood on your lips.
Or maybe it's the sun.

Testing your Strength

You thrust your hand, palm-turned
towards me, tell me to draw blood.

Your stubby nail-chewed fingers
know me, but I know I do not

want to squeeze anything from you.
You insist you need me

to measure your clotting time.
I hold my breath until I am no more

than someone extracting a pinhead,
making it grow, a snake's eye,

traffic light red and you
with your broad grin

spread it over your test
like butter on toast.

The Club

You say you have no childhood memories.
I say they form us anyway, create our needs.

I'm taking haylage to the rams in the lagoon enclosure.
The pond is hiding darkness under trees and clouds.

The rams are grazing the mound, half-eyeing the ewes.
These rams have black manes, proud noses, bow ties,

they are gods, arguing politics at their club and you are
with them, a heated debate on the role of the *Übermensch,*

all shoving and elbowing me to join the discussion,
then sticking tongues into my pocket for sheep nuts.

Kiss

In the yard an olive-brown stone
covered in bumps is skulking away.

Once a man took me boating on the Thames.
He wore a green tweed three-piece, a flat cap,
brought a wicker-hamper picnic,
we saw kingfishers.
With a dart of his hand, he caught a newt,
slipped it into his mouth.

Another crawled after me one dark night
clutched me from behind in passionate amplexus
croaking his love.

And here you come, all puffed up,
driving the quad as if you're at Goodwood.

O the toads I have kissed.

The Binding

With bolt-croppers and heavy-duty gloves
I head to the woods. You follow. On your phone.

These oaks have stood here for two hundred years,
they're home to buzzards, owls, sheltering deer,
the gall wasp, jewel beetle, purple hairstreak
butterfly. A fox shelters in the hollow of one.
Ages back someone wrapped them in wire.

You're reading the entire barbed history of wire.

I want to genuflect to the trees, say sorry
for piercings to their heartwood,
especially for wounds too deep to remove.

I loop the wire into manageable lengths,
twisted round the middle, make a pile,
transform it to sculpture,
the way painful things can seem beautiful.
Even the red line on my wrist.

Sometimes the wire has rusted in earth,
I tug and pull till it breaks. Some remains
underground.

You read: *barbed wire was so profitable*
it funded Campbell Crowne's trip to Antarctica,
though he later regretted the damage it caused.

I pause. It left me with an old scar:
Helena's 21st. Midsummer. I was Titania,
you, the donkey. We barely said *hi* in those days,
hearts don't do compromise.

The rays have made a glade of the wood,
I can see a hare statued among bluebells –
the smell of them is said to cast spells.
The juice of bluebells links love and death.

Last night I dreamt you were dead.
This does not mean I love you.

The Lyrids

I leave you asleep and creep to the yard
bare feet in boots and the entire universe

above: it's the night of a meteor shower.
I'm waiting for the dazzling display

of shooting stars and the lyric harp
for this dark to be alive with light, but

stillness comes when we least want it
and only the animals stir. I flash my torch

over their field ablaze with eyes as if Aries
has fallen to earth, and the silence grows

Greek-chorus loud from their bleating.
So much expression from just one sound.

I move away, humming. The sheep go quiet.
What if you and I tried talking in *Oms*?

She flies alone

The barn owl spreads herself
over the far field, searching
for mice, vole, mole and shrew,
swallows them whole,
spews out what can't be digested,
returns to the woods.

Today you say my smile has gone
weird. I'm not able to tell you
I have trespassed
into fields that aren't safe.
I'm drifting in the dark,
vomiting in secret.

waggle dance

she looks on throne-bored
dreams of taking to the sky but
it's hard to fly with wings tied
by lovers she cannot rid
even if she flew as far as Australia
the air would still fill with the hum
of them and the smell of hawthorn
sickly sweet and stale sex

What the sheep taught me 1

All day I have watched the ewes,
trying to see as they do, everything at once.
I think best sequentially:
it's getting towards evening.
The sheep know this too,
they're starting their sunset corral
of the field perimeter,
practising for the national,
leaping like antelope,
even the large one bearing triplets,
she soars over the electric fence,
she's made of spring.

All those fences I could have jumped.
I take a run. The shock sends me flying.

accident of birth

hunched in blackness
on a leafless tree it drops

with a ravenous rasp
for the tongue   the eyes
gores a hole in the fleece
of the newborn for the lungs
returns
snaps its long beak
watches   waits

       & the mother calling   calling
       & her lamb gasping   gasping
       & when it's removed
       for days she remains
       where she gave birth

clearing the brambles

fire of bones
jagging the sky
with silk kites
orange   red
smell of death
fox-crow-rat
being roasted

smoke wisps
craves invisibility
this lightness
attracts me
the way it shifts
refuses to be held
becomes nothing

I want to breath it in
even these charred bones
want to absorb all this
fox-crow-ratness
they just live
exactly
who they are

demands

it's the night when witches fly.
when the moon's too close, too full.

she is weighed down like a worrier,
an actress playing multiple roles.

when i came here she was wolf,
she was crow. soon she'll be blue,

she'll be flower, especially rose
then milk and corn planting.

providing, providing, so little support.
three days a month are not enough.

all these demands on her time.
no wonder she's cloud-hidden,

dreaming up pithy slogans, reflecting
on her rights, planning strikes.

The sky holds only silence and clouds

It's not you   it's ~~not~~ me   or maybe
I am a chameleon   playing at being
we don't talk   I drive you on

empty roads   winding through villages
everyone asleep   or hiding   or chameleon
before I leave   we walk on your beach

you tell me no one will ever love me
more   write my name in sand
I say the sea will wash it away

& scoop water into my hands   it slips
out   rejoins itself   as a wave
breathes sighs pauses   like my friend

who forgets to breathe when sleeping
one foot already crossing the threshold

drawn by fire

the guardian oak
at the entrance
has a lightning gash
all down its trunk
it is a miracle
the tree didn't catch fire

it is not true
that scar tissue
grows stronger
than ordinary skin
it just does its best
the branches look dead

soon its scars will be
hidden green

Rereading the evening

The road in is not the same
without you & with all this
time I am missing my books &
order more online stack them
into columns up to the ceiling
(the ceilings here are not high)
soon they will cover a wall a
bookcase on its side & I won't
need to feel guilty if I don't
read them as I can compose
stories from spines &
rearrange them to my mood:
men in the off hours / two cures for
love / the lost land / mad, sad &
bad / what if / another life / love
& I / split / dart / fast / joy

Ragwort and Cinnabar

Another email pings my inbox,
your ninth today and it's not yet lunchtime.

I never reply, but were I to hide,
you'd follow and find me, as if there's poison
in the heart of love.
                    Yesterday I was digging
up ragwort, trying to ignore the little fluttering
scarlet and black wings wanting the toxic
yellow flowers to revive.

Moths have been playing kamikaze all night
with my lamp as if seeking enlightenment,
while I sit thinking about Greenland's ice sheet,
facing a similar truth, open a window
and speak to the dark.

Messages

You keep texting and calling. I don't reply,
as Helena's arrived and I make coffee, and soon
she and I are talking about bookclubs and sheep,
though really I'm back there, revising for finals,
on the carpet, poring over Gothic Perpendicular,
thinking about him fucking her on the floor below
and hardly notice you come in and sit on me,
wanting to do what they're doing, and I let you,
but my mind is on what's happening downstairs
and the stained glass in York, where he's from.
Later I heard it didn't work and he died anyway.

Helena's giving me a look that says she wants
what I have, so I refill her cup, still not sure
why she's come, then catch his shadow behind her,
like Hugh Grant saying *Hi,* and I blink, wondering
why we see things that aren't there, why I'd let you
back when I never wanted you in the first place.

Still Life

I'm holding the ewe's head as her lambs
are removed one after another.
She has the eyes of an empress.
I stroke the fine hair on her cheeks,
as she gulps, unblinking, swallows,
mouth muscles twitching, and
her lips part with one *baa*.
I recognise the pain in the sound.

The lambs lie perfect and still,
sculpted alabaster or
a *plein air* artist arranging a palette:
lead white, raw umber, purple and
the cadmiums, yellow, orange, red.
The newborns are cellophane-wrapped,
inside see-through balloons,
someone will breathe life into them,
they are sleeping and when they wake
they'll jump with the other lambs.

The flies are arriving,
landing on the allantois
like people crowding an accident,
gawping.

What the sheep taught me 2

Sheep invented 'follow my leader'.
See how they charge to the new field
like a wake chasing a boat.
Even the ewe giving birth is running,
a little head bobbing under her tail.
They form in-crowds and outcasts
like at a cocktail party, polite
at first, calmly grazing, then shoving
each other, bitching, gossiping.

To say all sheep are the same
is a mother who finds no difference
between her children: we were
mostly good, unremarkable,
all called Child.

journeying home

once i tried jumping over fire/ threw
into it everything i wanted to be
rid of/ wrote things on sticks/ like
your name/ i tripped/ my therapist
asked what i was afraid of/ i said
nothing/ i was feeling strong that
day// now i'm fanning embers to
burn my bad/ the flames are the
sound of an old ciné projector/ a
film in reverse/ not stopping at birth
but spinning back/ spiralling in
space/ into a hole of such blackness/
an eye/ a gravity sink/ the tug of
home/ as if it were my choice to
come/ to read my own map//

The Nursery of Rejects

The newborn girl shivers
in her brown coat, ruby cord dangling,
edges forwards to be smelled, but
is head-butted, sent somersaulting.

Her brother, near-identical,
is licked all over,
the mother's staccato bleats
as she nuzzles, and he suckles.

The ewe lamb stamps her baby hoof
when I force in a teat, refuses the bottle.
I feel her rapid heartbeat.
So much unseen. Like that experiment
proving we need love and touch.
I hold her close, really close,
stroke her velvet black ears.

Things our mothers didn't tell us

Yesterday three lambs were taken.
A hen lay dead. Ten ducklings vanished.
I called the fox man.
Later he saw a hare leap through the field.

One night I was driving through a storm
my headlights fell on a brown scrap,
the size, but wrong shape, for a rat.
I pulled over, despite the rain,
a voice in my head said, *find a stone,*
put it out of its pain.

Our eyes met. It blinked,
and I lifted it. It was no more
than the size of my hand.
Most of it was ear. Ludicrous
ears. Sodden and still
yet a moth-wing heart.
I stroked it until warm
it moved its limbs and
I laid it on the hedgerow,
returned in the morning.
No sign it was there.

on the last day

two crows are charming a lamb, fly off
with a chuckle at my shepherd's crook.

in this story we all live from our lost
trees and stones. all that richness deep

down. the platinum and gold of earth's core.
here the sky makes me small.

there's a chance, about one in two thousand
asteroid *bennu* will hit earth.

if the solar system were squeezed into one day
humans would have had just three breaths.

in the past ten weeks i've taken three breaths
two million times. i am part of the farm.

the sheep and trees are in me. the wind is rising,
blowing straight through me. i can hear the sea.

Hymn to Sheep

O lamb, your gentleness daily sacrificed
yet muzzled, as if your ability to see
everything at once helps to let life pass.

yahn, tayn, tether, mether, mumph

O lamb who yearned to be a scholar until lost
by children: Bo Peep, Boy Blue.
Shepherds know humans don't do well on their own.

hither, lither, auver, dauver, dic

O sheep, how you group-gather, spin a yarn,
jaw-wagging, bleating, waving ears and tails,
and sheepishly laugh at your own jokes.

yahndic, tayndic, tetherdic, metherdic, mumphit

O sacred ruminants, so close to humans, once
mummified, valued ungulates, let me count you.
I shall finger my prayer-stones, will away my dark.

yahna mumphit, tayna mumphit, tethera mumphit

O ruminants what keeps you keeping on, knowing
one day that lorry will come for you? Is it just
your hope that grass might change colour?

methera mumphit, jigif and back to *yahn*

Acknowledgements

'Kiss' was first published by *London Grip*, 2022

'Still Life' was commended in the 2020 Winchester Poetry Prize and is published in The Winchester Poetry Prize Anthology, 2020

A version of 'She Flies Alone' was published as 'By Any Name' in *The High Window,* 2020

A version of 'Things our mothers didn't tell us' was published in *All About Our Mothers*, Nine Pens, 2022

'Hymn to Sheep' was highly commended in the *The Rialto* 'Nature and Place' Prize and will be published in the *The Rialto*, 2022

Thanks

First to William and Shay, for trusting me to farm-sit and for letting me stay during first lockdown; to my wonderful poet friends, you know who you are, and my workshop groups: Red Door Poets, the Crocodile Collective, Covent Garden Stanza and the Canada Water group; to Helen and the Live Canon team for making this pamphlet a reality; last, but far from least, to the Barbados Blackbelly sheep.